Cambodia
Travel Guide

Your Companion to Explore
The Kingdom of Wonder

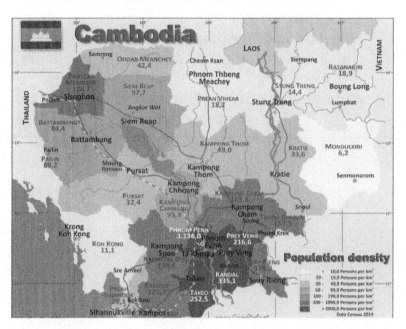

Meredith Biggs

Map of Cambodia

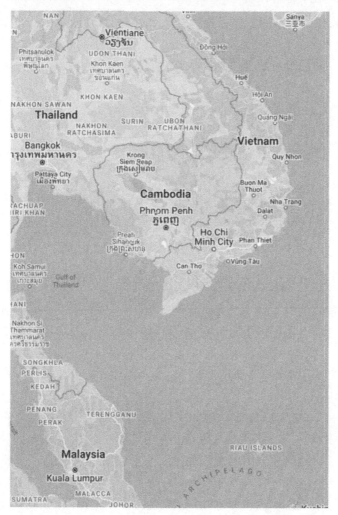

Table of Contents

Introduction

Welcome to the "Cambodia Travel Guide," your passport to one of the most enchanting and diverse destinations in Southeast Asia. Cambodia, often referred to as the "Kingdom of Wonder," beckons with a treasure trove of natural beauty, captivating history, vibrant culture, and warm hospitality. This guide is your compass to navigate the rich tapestry of experiences that this extraordinary nation has to offer.

Cambodia's crowning jewel, the ancient city of Angkor, has captivated the imagination of travelers for centuries. With its mystical temples, including the iconic Angkor Wat, and sprawling ruins nestled amidst lush jungles, this UNESCO World Heritage site is a testament to the ingenuity and grandeur of the Khmer Empire. As you explore this archaeological marvel, you'll step back in time and walk in the footsteps of emperors and monks, unlocking the secrets of a civilization lost to history.

Beyond the temples, Cambodia offers a myriad of activities for the adventurous traveler. Whether you're seeking heart-pounding thrills in the

Cardamom Mountains, cruising along the tranquil waters of the Mekong River, or discovering hidden gems in the bustling markets of Phnom Penh, there's an adventure for every taste. Cambodia's natural beauty, from the picturesque landscapes of Kep's pepper plantations to the untouched beaches of Sihanoukville, provides the perfect backdrop for hiking, snorkeling, and unwinding on pristine shores.

The culinary scene in Cambodia is a journey in itself. Khmer cuisine, with its delicate balance of flavors and fragrances, is a delightful fusion of influences from neighboring countries.

Savor delicious dishes like fish amok, a creamy and fragrant curry, or sample the bold flavors of street food. From bustling markets to elegant riverside restaurants, Cambodia's culinary landscape is a sensory experience not to be missed.

For those with a penchant for culinary exploration, Cambodia's diverse cuisine offers a world of flavors to discover. From the delectable "kuy teav" noodle soup served at humble roadside stalls to the fiery "lok lak" stir-fry, you'll embark on a culinary adventure that reflects the country's varied regions and influences.

The heart of Cambodia beats with its unique cultural traditions. From the graceful Apsara dancers who bring ancient stories to life to the captivating tales spun through shadow puppetry, the country's cultural richness is on full display. Don't miss the opportunity to learn about Cambodia's storied history through museums and historical sites, including the sobering reminders of the Khmer Rouge regime at the Killing Fields and Tuol Sleng Genocide Museum.

The natural beauty of Cambodia is a tapestry of lush landscapes, serene rivers, and pristine coastlines. The Tonle Sap Lake, Southeast Asia's largest freshwater lake, offers a chance to explore floating villages and see life along the riverbanks. Meanwhile, the picturesque waterfalls of Kulen Mountain beckon adventurers, and the rainforests of the Cardamom Mountains are a sanctuary for wildlife enthusiasts.

As you embark on your journey through the pages of this Cambodia Travel Guide, you'll find yourself immersed in the heart of a country where the past meets the present, where every temple, every market, and every landscape carries a story waiting to be told. Cambodia invites you to explore its mysteries, connect with its people, and uncover the hidden gems that lie off the beaten path. So, fasten your seatbelt and prepare for a transformative adventure, where the wonders of the past and the magic of the present coexist in perfect harmony, in a land often described as the "Kingdom of Wonder."

Welcome to Cambodia

Welcome to Cambodia, a land where the past gracefully dances with the present, and where the warmth of its people is as inviting as its breathtaking landscapes. From the ancient wonders of Angkor Wat to the vibrant streets of Phnom Penh, Cambodia beckons travelers to explore its rich tapestry of history, culture, and natural beauty.

In the heart of Southeast Asia, Cambodia reveals the stories of its glorious Khmer Empire through intricate temple ruins, each whispering tales of grandeur and resilience. Yet, this nation is not just a museum of history; it's a thriving, resilient country that has overcome the darkest of chapters and emerged with a spirit that's as unbreakable as the temples themselves.

Cambodia's diverse landscapes, from lush jungles and pristine beaches to the meandering Mekong River, offer endless adventures. Its cultural heritage, deeply rooted in Buddhism and traditional arts, enchants visitors with vibrant festivals and timeless rituals. And let's not forget the enchanting cuisine, where flavors burst forth with aromatic spices and exotic ingredients, leaving an indelible mark on every traveler's palate.

Welcome to a land of smiles and stories, where every step leads to a new, awe-inspiring chapter in your own adventure.

Quick Facts about Cambodia

Here are some quick facts about Cambodia:

- Official name:Kingdom of Cambodia
- Capital: Phnom Penh
- Population: 16.7 million (2021 estimate)
- Language: Khmer
- Religion: Buddhism (95%)
- Currency: Cambodian riel (KHR)
- Climate: Tropical
- Government: Constitutional monarchy

- Independence: November 9, 1953 (from France)
- Cambodia is home to over 1,000 rivers and streams.
- The Tonle Sap Lake, located in Cambodia, is the largest freshwater lake in Southeast Asia.
- Cambodia is home to a variety of wildlife, including tigers, elephants, and leopards
- The Cambodian people are known for their kindness and hospitality.
- Cambodia is a developing country, but it has made significant progress in recent years.

Discovering Cambodia

Geography, Climate and Population

Geography

Cambodia is located in the southwest of the Indochinese peninsula, with borders to the west and northwest, Laos to the northeast, Vietnam to the east, and the Gulf of Thailand to the southwest. It covers an area of 181,035 square km.

Cambodia's physical coordinates are 13 00 N and 105 00 E.

The flat plains cover the majority of Cambodia, with mountains to the north and southwest.

The Tonlé Sap Lake and the Mekong River, which flows from north to south across Cambodia, are two of the country's most significant natural features.

Natural resources include oil and gas, wood, gemstones, iron ore, manganese, phosphates, and hydropower potential.

Population

Cambodia's population is estimated to be at 15 million people. Ninety percent of the population is Chinese, Vietnamese, Indian, Thai, Phnong, Kuoy, Stieng, Tamil, Cham (the Khmer Muslim group), and others. The population density per square kilometer is 78.

Climate

Cambodia, like the rest of Southeast Asia, has year-round heat and humidity. The ecology is dominated by the yearly monsoon cycle, which alternates between rainy and dry seasons. The wet season lasts from May to October, and the dry season lasts from November to April. The coldest months are December through January, while the hottest month is April. The temperature ranges between 27 and 28 degrees Celsius on average.

History and Culture

History

Similar to modern-day Cambodian communities along the Mekong, the Khmer people are said to have been among the first people to live in Southeast Asia about the first century CE. They produced rice and fished from stilted houses. They are also said to have absorbed political and religious ideals from India, their neighbour.

The first independent Khmer state, Chenla, also known as Kambuja, gained notoriety in the sixth century and was ruled by Jayavarman I. Following many years of instability, the lands that would eventually form the Khmer Empire were progressively brought together under the leadership of Jayavarman II, the first monarch of the greatest dynasty to ever rule Southeast Asia.

For the next few centuries, the Khmer civilization—also known as the Angkor Empire—continued to exist. Even though there was still infighting at the conclusion of this era, art and architecture reached their peak once Suryavarman II reclaimed the throne and united the nation. In Khmer tradition, Suryavarman is regarded with affection as the king who gave the order to build Angkor Wat. The great reformer Jayavarman VI's rule in the 12th century marked the height of Angkor's cultural and political influence.

After his death, internal warfare between the higher classes of the monarchy and religion gradually tore Angkor apart, returning the empire to pre-war patterns. The crumbling empire staggered along until 1431, when the once-dominant Angkor Thom was besieged by the Thai civilization, a new regional force and current adversary.

Between the fifteenth and nineteenth centuries, Cambodia was subjected to despicable rulers who sought to retain their thrones as a shield against increasingly powerful neighbours Siam (Thailand) and Vietnam. The land swayed back and forth between these two kingdoms' protection. But as Europe's superpowers asserted themselves in Asia, the political scene again changed.

Three years after taking the throne in 1860, Norodom I of Cambodia was forced to establish a protectorate with France. This, in theory, kept the kingdom from being engulfed by its neighbours. But after twenty years, Cambodia had essentially become another French Indochina colony. Even though the colonial rulers did nothing to better the lot of the Cambodians, Siem Reap was taken back from Siam, returning control of the important Angkor Wat to the Cambodian people, and the royalty was once again revered.

The outbreak of World War II and its eventual conclusion forced France to lose control of its Asian possessions and enter the Vietnam War, which provided Cambodia with its first taste of independence. When Cambodia attained independence in late 1953, led by a young King Sihanouk, years of reform and what some have dubbed the country's "Golden Era" following. The arts and culture blossomed in Phnom Penh, and Angkor Wat rose to prominence as one of Southeast Asia's leading tourist sites. Nonetheless, in typical Cambodian fashion, instability resurfaced fast, and by 1970, revolution was undeniably here.

Within months of the army overthrowing the king in a coup led by Lieutenant General Prime Minister Lon Nol, infighting resumed. Several parties, most notably the Khmer Rouge, also known as the Communist Party of Kampuchea, rebelled against the new government commanded by Lon Nol. The Khmer Rouge, commanded by Pol Pot and a new generation of socialists educated in Paris, forced the government out of Phnom Penh in 1975 and immediately began creating their new regime.

Banking systems were destroyed, religion was prohibited,

communication with the outside world was halted, and cities were abandoned. Almost the whole population was assigned to work in the fields as part of a new, revolutionary agrarian system. During the next four years, the fanatical and brutal Khmer Rouge carried out one of the deadliest atrocities of the twenty-first century, killing an estimated 1.2 to 1.6 million Cambodians between 1975 and 1979.

In the final years of its awful rule, the Khmer Rouge began invading Vietnamese regions, prompting a full-scale Vietnamese military invasion of Cambodia over Christmas 1978. Only two weeks later, Pol Pot and his regime were deposed. However, the people of this broken nation suffered for the next ten years, with a civil war that lasted until the 1990s. Following peace talks in 1992, the United Nations Transitional Authority in Cambodia took power and held the country's first constitutionally recognised election, paving the way for a steady and cautious recovery.

Culture

Family and religion are the two main pillars of Cambodian culture. Though throughout the early years religion changed from Hinduism to Buddhism, the latter solidified in the 13th century and now constitutes the faith of almost 90% of the population. There is a shrine of some type in almost every house and business in the nation, where regular offerings are made, usually for good fortune.

The culture places great importance on family and social hierarchy, wherein both senior family members and elderly strangers are accorded great respect. Respect is expressed when one bows and puts one's hands together in the traditional Cambodian greeting, known as the sampan. Families usually live next door or in the same house, and community living is rather common, particularly in rural areas.

Cambodian culture places a high value on clothing, and traditional attire is still commonly worn. The most famous article of apparel from Cambodia is the karma. This ingenious piece of cloth can be worn as a sunhat, a towel, a kid's hammock, or just as a stylish piece of clothing. Despite the fact that both sexes now dress normally in western clothing, both men and women still choose to cover their lower bodies with the bright material known as a sampan. Even now, people wear dresses like these on important occasions like weddings.

The most famous thing of Cambodia is its aspara (nymph) dance, which originated during the height of the Angkor Empire. The dancers in Aspara are usually clothed in traditional, lave clothing, and the style of the dance is noted for its unique use of the hands and feet to convey the mood of the piece. Even though the Khmer Rouge regime significantly reduced the output of literature, music, and film, these mediums are now slowly returning to contemporary culture thanks to a resurgence of 1960s bands and motion pictures.

Language and Customs

Language

The official language of Cambodia is Khmer. Khmer is a Mon-Khmer language, which means that it is related to other languages spoken in Southeast Asia, such as Vietnamese and Lao. Khmer is spoken by over 16 million people, the majority of whom live in Cambodia.

Khmer is a tonal language, meaning that the meaning of a word can change depending on the tone used to pronounce it. Khmer also has a complex system of consonants and vowels.

Customs of Cambodia

Cambodia has a rich and unique culture, and there are a number of customs that visitors should be aware of.

- Greetings: When greeting someone in Cambodia, it is customary to shake their hand and say "chumnum teb" (hello). If you are greeting someone older or more respected than you, it is customary to bow slightly.

- Dress: It is important to dress modestly in Cambodia, especially when visiting temples and other religious sites. Avoid wearing shorts, tank tops, or revealing clothing.

- Religion: Cambodia is a predominantly Buddhist country, and it is important to respect the Buddhist religion. Avoid touching Buddhist monks or nuns, and do not sit higher than them.

- Gift-giving: If you are invited to a Cambodian home, it is customary to bring a small gift, such as fruit, flowers, or sweets.

Here are some additional tips for respecting Cambodian customs:

- Be polite and respectful: Cambodians are known for their politeness and respect. Be sure to be polite and respectful when interacting with Cambodians.
- Be patient: Cambodians are generally laid-back and

easygoing. Be patient if things don't run on time or if things don't go exactly as planned.

- Be open-minded: Cambodia has a rich and unique culture. Be open-minded and respectful of Cambodian customs and traditions.

Economy and Society

The Cambodian economy is a lower-middle-income economy that is heavily reliant on agriculture, tourism, and the garment industry. The economy has grown rapidly in recent years, but it is still vulnerable to external shocks.

- Agriculture is the backbone of the Cambodian economy, accounting for about 30% of GDP and employing over 70% of the workforce. The main agricultural products are rice, rubber, cassava, and maize.

- Tourism is another important sector of the Cambodian economy, accounting for about 15% of GDP and employing over 1 million people. The main tourist destinations include the Angkor

Wat temple complex, the beaches of Sihanoukville, and the Tonle Sap Lake.

- The garment industry is the third-largest sector of the Cambodian economy, accounting for about 10% of GDP and employing over 700,000 people. The garment industry is mostly export-oriented, and the main export markets are the United States and the European Union.

Other important sectors of the Cambodian economy

include construction, energy, and mining.

- Cambodian society is characterized by a high level of inequality. The richest 10% of the population controls over 40% of the country's wealth. The poorest 20% of the population controls less than 5% of the country's wealth.

- Cambodia is a young country, with a median age of 25.5 years. The population is growing at a rate of about 1.5% per year.

- The majority of Cambodians are Buddhist. Buddhism plays an important role in Cambodian culture and society.

- Cambodia is a member of the Association of Southeast Asian Nations (ASEAN) and the World Trade Organization (WTO).

Cambodia Travel Guide

Planning Your Trip

Visa Requirements and Entry

Who Needs a Visa to Enter Cambodia?

Everyone who intends to travel to Cambodia must have a visa except passport holders of ASEAN countries:

Brunei (14 days)

Indonesia (30 days)

Laos (30 days)

Malaysia (30 days)

Philippines (21 days)

Seychelles (14 days)

Singapore (30 days)

Thailand (14 days)

Vietnam (30 days)

Fortunately, visas are accessible on arrival and online, and the process is rather simple.

Note: If you are from Afghanistan, Algeria, Bangladesh, Iran, Iraq, Pakistan, Saudi Arabia, Sri Lanka, Sudan, or Syria, you cannot apply for a Cambodia visa online. A visa can only be obtained on arrival or at an embassy.

What Are the Types of Cambodian Visas

Cambodia has two categories of visas: tourist and business.

- Visas for tourists (T). They are solely granted for tourism purposes.

- Ordinary visas (E). When you first acquire an ordinary (E) visa for Cambodia, it is valid for the same period as a tourist visa. However, depending on your purpose of travel, you can extend it while in Cambodia.

☐ Cambodia Business visa (EB), for business visitors or those working in Cambodia on a long-term basis. This visa can be extended for a period of up to one year.

☐ Cambodia Retirement visa (ER), for foreign people over the age of 55 who are retired and can financially support themselves without working. This visa can be extended for a period of up to one year.

☐ Cambodia Student Visa (ES), granted to international students who have been accepted into a Cambodian educational institution. This visa can be extended for a period of up to one year.

☐ Cambodia Job-seeking visa (EG), for foreign nationals looking for work in Cambodia. This visa can be extended for a period of up to six months.

☐ Cambodia Multiple entry visas are E visas that have been extended for more than 30 days.

How to Apply for a Cambodia Visa?

You can apply for a Cambodia visa through one of the following methods

- Online (Cambodia eVisa). You can only enter through specific airports/land borders.
- On arrival – at an airport or border crossing.
- At an Embassy of Cambodia abroad.

Obtaining eVisa

You must apply for the Cambodia eVisa using the Cambodian Foreign Affairs Services' official website. The only

Cambodian visa that may be obtained online is the tourist visa (T class).

- Begin the application procedure by visiting the official government website.
- You can pay the application cost using a debit or credit card. A Cambodia eVisa costs US$30 plus a US$6 processing fee.
- Allow for the processing of the visa. This will take approximately three days.
- Receive confirmation of your Cambodia eVisa.

- Travel to Cambodia and provide your confirmation to the immigration agents at the border.

You can enter Cambodia using Visa through one of the following entry ports:

- Phnom Penh International Airport
- Siem Reap International Airport
- Preah Sihanouk International Airport
- Cham Yeam (Koh Kong) – Thailand border
- Poi Pet (Banteay Meanchey) – Thailand border
- Bavet (Svay Rieng) – Vietnam border

- Tropaeng Kreal Border Post (Stung Treng) – Laos Border

How Do I Get a Cambodia Visa on Arrival?

You can apply for a Cambodia visa on arrival for either tourism (T class) or business (EB visa) purposes:

- Fill out an immigration card that you will be given on the plane. If you do not receive an immigration card on the flight, you can obtain one at the airport/entry point.
- Queue at the visa-on-arrival application counter. There will

generally be a sign directing you to the application centre at the airport/entry point.

- Present your passport, immigration card, passport-sized photos, return flight ticket, and enough cash to cover the visa price. Visa on Arrival costs $30 for a tourist visa and $35 for a business visa. You must pay in cash in US dollars.
- Wait a few moments for the immigration authorities to process your visa application.
- Before stamping your visa on your passport, the immigration official

will also take your picture and
fingerprints.

You can get a Cambodian visa on arrival
at one of the following entry points:

      i.   Phnom   Penh
            International
            Airport

     ii.   Siem   Reap
            International
            Airport

- Vietnam border:

☐ Banteay Chakrey International
Border Check Point

☐ Bavet International Check Point

- ☐ Kha Orm Sam Nor International Check Point
- ☐ Oyadav International CheckPoint
- ☐ Phnom Den International Check Point
- ☐ Prek Chak International Check Point
- ☐ Samrong International Check Point
- ☐ Tropeang Sre International Check Point
- ☐ Tropieng Phlong International Check Point

- • Thailand border:
- ☐ Anglong Veng International Check Point

- ☐ Cham Yeam International Check Point
- ☐ Doung International Check Point
- ☐ Osmach International Check Point
- ☐ Poi Pet International Check Point
- ☐ Prum International Check Point

- Laos border:
- ☐ Dong Krolar International Check Point

How to Apply for a Cambodia Visa at a Consulate?

You can apply for a Cambodian visa at one of Cambodia's diplomatic missions overseas, such as an Embassy or Consulate:

- Find the nearest Embassy or Consulate. The official website contains a list of Cambodian embassies and consulates.
- To learn more about the visa application procedure and requirements, contact the Embassy/Consulate or visit its website.
- Gather the necessary paperwork. A list of documents is usually available on the website.

- Depending on their unique criteria, go to the Embassy/Consulate in person or send the application by mail.

What Documents Do I Need for a Visa to Cambodia?

When applying for a Cambodia visa, you must bring the following documents:

- Your passport, which must be valid for at least six months more and have at least one blank visa page
- A return flight ticket.

- Pay the visa fee in US dollars (US$30 for a tourist visa; US$35 for a regular visa).
- When submitting an application to an embassy: Other documents required by immigration agents, such as a cover letter, invitation letter, etc.
- Your passport-sized photograph.
- After you are in Cambodia, you will need additional documents, depending on the sort of extension you require, such as an employment contract, proof of enrolment in a Cambodian school, and so on.

Is it Possible to Extend a Cambodian Visa?

Yes, all Cambodian visas, both tourist and ordinary, can be extended:

- A tourist visa to Cambodia can only be extended once for another 30 days at the Immigration Department of the Cambodian National Police.

- Ordinary (E) visas can be extended for 1, 3, 6, or 12 months at the Immigration Department of the Cambodian National Police, depending on your needs. When you extend your visa, you must have all required documentation pertaining to your purpose in Cambodia with you. If you are going to work, you will need a job contract/letter; if you are going to study, you will need a letter of enrollment, and so on.

Best Time to Visit

The best time to visit Cambodia is during the **dry season**, which runs from **November to April**. During this time, the weather is generally sunny and warm, with little rainfall. This makes it ideal for sightseeing, exploring temples, and enjoying the outdoors.

The **wet season** in Cambodia runs from **May to October**. During this time, the weather is hot and humid, with heavy rainfall in the afternoons. This can make it difficult to get around and enjoy the outdoors, but it can also be a good time to visit if you're looking for cheaper deals on accommodation and activities.

The best time to visit Cambodia, depending on your interests:

- Sightseeing: The best time for sightseeing is during the dry season, when the weather is clear and sunny.

- Temple exploring: The best time to explore temples is also during the dry season, when the weather is comfortable and there are fewer crowds.

- Beaches: The best time to visit the beach is during the dry season, when the weather is warm and sunny and the water is clear.

- Festivals: Cambodia has a number of festivals throughout the year, so you may want to plan your trip around one of these if you're interested in experiencing Cambodian culture.

Budgeting and Costs

Cambodia is a relatively inexpensive country to visit, but the cost of your trip will vary depending on your travel style and budget. Here is a breakdown of some of the costs you can expect:

- Accommodation: Accommodation in Cambodia ranges from budget guesthouses to luxury hotels. You can expect to pay around $10-$15 per night for a budget guesthouse, $20-$30 per night for a mid-range hotel, and $50+ per night for a luxury hotel.

- Food: Food is also relatively inexpensive in Cambodia. You can expect to pay around $5-$10 per day for food, depending on your eating habits. If you eat at street stalls and local restaurants, you can save even more money.

- Transportation: Transportation in Cambodia is also relatively inexpensive. You can get around by tuk-tuk, bus, or taxi. A tuk-tuk ride costs around $1-$2 for a short ride, and a bus ride costs around $5-$10 for a long-distance ride.

- Activities: The cost of activities in Cambodia will vary depending on what you want to do. For example, a visit to the Angkor Wat temple complex costs $37 for a one-day pass, $62 for a three-day pass, and $72 for a seven-day pass. Other activities, such as boat trips and cooking classes, can also be expensive.

Here is a sample budget for a 7-day trip to Cambodia:

* Accommodation: $105
* Food: $210
* Transportation: $70

* Activities: $210

* Total: $595

The Capital: Phnom Penh

Overview of Phnom Penh

Phnom Penh is the capital and largest city of Cambodia. It is located on the banks of the Mekong and Tonle Sap rivers, and has a population of over 2 million people. Phnom Penh is a vibrant and cosmopolitan city, with a rich history and culture.

The city was founded in the 15th century by King Ponhea Yat, and was the capital of the Khmer Empire during its golden age. Phnom Penh was also the capital of French Cambodia during the colonial era, and became the capital of independent Cambodia in 1953.

The city was severely damaged during the Khmer Rouge regime, but has since been rebuilt. Today, Phnom Penh is a thriving city with a growing economy. It is a popular tourist destination, known for its temples, palaces, and museums.

Here are some of the things to see and do in Phnom Penh:

- Royal Palace: The Royal Palace is the official residence of the King of Cambodia. It is a complex of buildings that includes the Silver Pagoda, which houses a collection of Khmer art and artifacts.

- Silver Pagoda: The Silver Pagoda is located within the Royal Palace complex. It is home to a collection of Khmer art and artifacts, including the Emerald Buddha and the Golden Buddha.

- National Museum of Cambodia: The National Museum of Cambodia houses a collection of Khmer art and artifacts from the Angkorian period to the present day.

- Tuol Sleng Genocide Museum: The Tuol Sleng Genocide Museum is a former school that was used as a torture and execution center by the Khmer Rouge regime. It is a sobering reminder of the atrocities committed during the Khmer Rouge period.

- Choeung Ek Killing Fields: The Choeung Ek Killing Fields is a former orchard that was used as a mass grave by the Khmer Rouge regime. It is a sobering reminder of the atrocities committed during the Khmer Rouge period.

- Russian Market: The Russian Market is a popular market where you can buy souvenirs, handicrafts, and clothing.

- Central Market: The Central Market is another popular market where you can buy fresh produce, meat, and seafood.

Must-See Landmarks and Monuments

Here are guide notes on a selection of these significant sites:

1. Royal Palace and Silver Pagoda:

- The Royal Palace is a mesmerizing architectural masterpiece that serves as the official residence of the Cambodian monarch. Its golden spires, intricate design, and lush gardens create a captivating visual spectacle.

- Within the Royal Palace complex, you'll discover the Silver Pagoda, known for its stunning silver floor tiles and an impressive emerald Buddha statue. The pagoda is a true testament to Cambodia's rich heritage.

2. Wat Phnom:

- Wat Phnom, situated on a small hill, is the city's namesake. It's a peaceful and spiritual place that offers respite from the bustling streets of Phnom Penh.

- This temple complex, adorned with colorful murals and intricate statues, is a testament to the enduring faith of the Cambodian people.

3. Tuol Sleng Genocide Museum (S-21):

- While not a traditional tourist attraction, the Tuol Sleng Genocide

Museum is a powerful and somber reminder of Cambodia's tragic history under the Khmer Rouge regime. Once a high school, it was transformed into a detention and torture center.

- The museum tells the heart-wrenching stories of the victims through photographs, testimonials, and preserved cells, shedding light on a period that Cambodia has courageously confronted and overcome.

4. Choeung Ek Killing Fields:

- A visit to the Choeung Ek Killing Fields complements the experience at the Tuol Sleng Museum. It's a stark but important destination that pays homage to the victims of the Khmer Rouge.

- The memorial stupa, housing thousands of skulls, stands as a powerful symbol of remembrance and reflection.

5. Independence Monument:

- The Independence Monument, designed in the architectural style of a lotus-shaped stupa, stands as a symbol of Cambodia's liberation from French colonial rule in 1953.

- Illuminated at night, the monument is a sight to behold, and the surrounding park is a popular spot for both locals and visitors.

6. National Museum of Cambodia:

- The National Museum is a treasure trove of Cambodian art and history. Its red terracotta structure houses an extensive collection of sculptures, ceramics, and artifacts, dating back to the Angkorian period.

- The museum is a fascinating educational experience, offering insights into the country's artistic and cultural evolution.

7. Central Market (Phsar Thmei):

- Not just a landmark, but also a vibrant market, Phsar Thmei is an architectural gem with its distinctive art deco design and a massive central dome.

- Here, you can shop for traditional Khmer crafts, jewelry, clothing, and an array of local products.

Museums and Cultural Institutions

Here, we will delve into some of these iconic sites in Phnom Penh:

1. The Royal Palace (Preah Barum Reachea Veang Nei): The Royal Palace is a masterpiece of Khmer architecture, a symbol of Cambodia's enduring

monarchy. Its ornate spires and glistening roofs house stunning treasures, including the Silver Pagoda, which boasts a floor made of over 5,000 silver tiles and a life-sized gold Buddha. The manicured gardens and richly decorated buildings make the Royal Palace an architectural marvel and a must-visit.

2. Silver Pagoda (Wat Preah Keo Morokat): This temple, situated within the Royal Palace complex, is renowned for its dazzling silver floors, housing a stunning collection of precious Buddhist and historical objects, including the famous Emerald Buddha

and an astonishing 90-kilogram gold Buddha statue. The intricate murals and breathtaking architecture make this temple a significant cultural and religious site.

3. The National Museum of Cambodia: Located just north of the Royal Palace, this elegant terracotta structure houses an exceptional collection of Khmer art and historical artifacts. With over 14,000 items, the museum is a treasure trove of sculptures, ceramics, bronzes, and more, providing a deep dive into Cambodia's artistic heritage.

4. Wat Phnom: The namesake of the city, Wat Phnom is perched on a small hill and offers not only a beautiful temple but also a serene park-like setting, making it a popular spot for both locals and tourists to unwind and enjoy some tranquility. The temple's legend is fascinating, as it's believed that a wealthy widow named Penh discovered four statues of Buddha and founded the temple on this hill.

5. Independence Monument: A symbol of Cambodia's independence from French colonial rule in 1953, the Independence Monument is an iconic landmark in Phnom Penh. The

lotus-shaped stupa stands tall in the heart of the city, particularly impressive when illuminated at night.

6. Choeung Ek Genocidal Center (Killing Fields): While not a joyful site, the Killing Fields are an essential stop for those seeking to understand Cambodia's tragic history uring the Khmer Rouge regime. The memorial stupa at Choeung Ek contains thousands of human skulls, serving as a poignant reminder of the atrocities committed during that dark period. It's a somber but crucial visit to honor the victims and learn about Cambodia's resilience.

7. Tuol Sleng Genocide Museum (S-21 Prison): Located in a former school, this museum documents the horrors of the Khmer Rouge era. The stark and chilling exhibits provide a haunting glimpse into the regime's brutality and its impact on the people of Cambodia.

8. Phnom Penh Riverside: A leisurely stroll along the picturesque Tonlé Sap River is a wonderful way to experience the heart of the city. You can admire the Royal Palace and the Silver Pagoda on one side and see bustling street life and local markets on the other.

Dining and Nightlife

Dining and nightlife in Phnom Penh, Cambodia, offer an eclectic mix of flavors and entertainment, making it a vibrant and evolving scene that caters to diverse tastes. Let's delve into the dining experiences, nightlife options, and the unique blend of local and international influences that characterize Phnom Penh's culinary and after-dark landscape.

Dining in Phnom Penh:

1. Khmer Cuisine: Cambodian cuisine is a delightful fusion of flavors. Don't

miss classic dishes like Amok (a fragrant coconut milk curry), Lok Lak (stir-fried beef), and Fish Amok (a fish curry). For an authentic experience, dine at local eateries where you can savor traditional dishes.

2. Street Food: Phnom Penh's bustling street food scene is a must-experience. From savory grilled skewers to fresh tropical fruits, the streets are alive with culinary delights. Head to the Night Market or Phsar Chas for a genuine street food experience.

3. Riverside Dining: The Tonlé Sap River offers a beautiful backdrop for dining.

Riverside restaurants serve a variety of international and local dishes. Enjoy a sunset dinner while gazing at the illuminated Royal Palace and the bustling street life along the riverbank.

4. International Cuisine: The city caters to a global palate, with international restaurants offering everything from Italian and French to Japanese and Indian cuisine. You'll find a wide range of options that cater to expats and tourists.

5. Markets and Food Stalls: Vibrant markets like Central Market and Russian Market not only offer great

shopping but also a variety of local food stalls. Try some grilled meat skewers or fresh spring rolls while exploring the markets.

Nightlife in Phnom Penh:

1. Riverside Bars: The riverside comes alive at night with numerous bars and restaurants offering scenic views of the Tonlé Sap River. Whether you prefer a quiet drink or a lively night out, there's something for everyone.

2. Pub Street: Street 51, commonly known as 'Pub Street,' is the nightlife hub of Phnom Penh. Here, you'll find a

range of bars, clubs, and restaurants, each with its unique vibe. From sports bars to live music venues, it's the place to be for a night out.

3. Live Music: Phnom Penh has a vibrant live music scene. Enjoy local and international bands performing at venues like Oscar's on the Corner and Meta House. From rock to jazz, there's a diverse range of music to appreciate.

4. Rooftop Bars: Phnom Penh boasts several rooftop bars offering panoramic views of the city. Sip on cocktails while admiring the city lights and the shimmering Mekong River.

5. Late-Night Street Food : After a night of revelry, Phnom Penh's street food stalls come to the rescue. You can satisfy those late-night cravings with Khmer noodles, grilled meats, and other delicious treats.

6. Casinos: Phnom Penh is home to numerous casinos, offering a unique nightlife experience. NagaWorld, the largest integrated resort and casino, is a popular destination for those looking to try their luck.

Accommodation Options

Luxury Hotels and Resorts:

The "Raffles Grand Hotel d'Angkor" in Siem Reap is an iconic 5-star property that exudes old-world charm and offers an exceptional experience. Set within a historic colonial building, it features elegant suites, lush gardens, a stunning pool, and personalized services.

In Phnom Penh, "Rosewood Phnom Penh" is a modern luxury hotel that towers above the city, providing breathtaking views of the Mekong River. With sleek contemporary design, fine dining, and spa facilities, it's an oasis of comfort.

Boutique and Heritage Hotels:

Siem Reap's "The Pavilion" is a boutique hotel that offers guests the chance to stay in a traditional Khmer house. With its antique furnishings, tranquil courtyards, and lush gardens, it provides a serene and unique experience.

In Phnom Penh, "The Plantation" is a heritage hotel housed in a beautifully restored colonial mansion. It seamlessly blends history with modern amenities, offering a glimpse into Cambodia's past.

Mid-Range Hotels:

"Golden Temple Villa" in Siem Reap is a mid-range hotel with clean and comfortable rooms. It provides excellent value for travelers and includes a pool, a restaurant, and friendly staff.

"The Quay Boutique Hotel" in Phnom Penh is a stylish mid-range option located along the Tonlé Sap River. It offers modern rooms and a vibrant rooftop bar.

Hostels and Guesthouses:

"Mad Monkey Hostel" is a popular chain of hostels with locations in both Siem Reap and Phnom Penh. They offer affordable dormitory and private rooms, as well as a lively social atmosphere with bars, pools, and various activities.

"Eighty8 Backpackers" is a friendly and budget-friendly guesthouse in Sihanoukville, known for its relaxed vibe and convenient location near the beach.

Eco-Lodges:

"Cardamom Tented Camp" in the Cardamom Mountains offers an eco-friendly experience in luxury tents. Guests can immerse themselves in nature while contributing to conservation efforts.

"4 Rivers Floating Lodge" in Koh Kong provides eco-luxury in floating bungalows along the Tatai River. It's an ideal destination for those seeking both comfort and sustainability.

Homestays:

Various rural villages surrounding Battambang offer homestay experiences where travelers can live with local families, participate in daily activities, and gain insight into traditional Khmer life.

Floating Villages:

"Prek Toal Home Stay" near the Prek Toal bird sanctuary offers the unique experience of staying in a floating village on the Tonlé Sap Lake. Guests can witness the vibrant life of the lake communities.

Budget Accommodations:

"Lub d Cambodia Hostel" in Siem Reap is a stylish and budget-friendly hostel with dormitory rooms. It's known for its vibrant social atmosphere and modern design.

"Velkommen Guesthouse" in Phnom Penh offers simple and clean rooms at an affordable price, making it a practical choice for budget travelers.

Temples and Archaeological Sites

Angkor Wat and the Angkor Temples

Angkor Wat and the Angkor Temples are one of the most remarkable archaeological and historical sites in the world, nestled in the lush jungles of Cambodia. These ancient structures, often regarded as the epitome of Khmer architecture, tell a captivating story of the Khmer Empire's grandeur and legacy. Here, we'll take a deep dive into the awe-inspiring world of Angkor Wat and the surrounding temples.

Angkor Wat: The Jewel of Cambodia

- Architectural Marvel: Angkor Wat is the largest religious monument on Earth and represents a stunning example of Khmer architecture. Its intricate design, including intricate bas-reliefs and towering spires, is a testament to the skill and artistic achievements of the Khmer civilization.

- Spiritual Significance: Originally constructed as a Hindu temple dedicated to the god Vishnu, Angkor Wat later became a Buddhist site. The temple's alignment with cosmic principles and its symbolism are evident in its layout, which mirrors the universe in miniature.

- Intricate Bas-Reliefs: The temple is adorned with exquisite bas-reliefs that tell stories from Hindu epics, including the Ramayana and the Mahabharata. These carvings, which encircle the temple, provide insight into Khmer culture and history.

- Sunrise and Sunset: Angkor Wat is particularly famous for its stunning sunrise and sunset views. Travelers often gather to witness the temple's silhouette against the changing colors of the sky, creating a mesmerizing experience.

- Conservation and Preservation: Efforts have been made to conserve Angkor Wat, and it is a UNESCO World Heritage site. Care is taken to protect the temple's structural integrity and delicate carvings while allowing visitors to appreciate its magnificence.

The Angkor Temple Complex: A World of Wonders

- Angkor Thom: This massive city complex once served as the Khmer Empire's capital. The South Gate, flanked by serene stone faces, is one of its iconic features.

- Bayon Temple: Known for its numerous massive stone faces,

Bayon is a mysterious and enchanting temple that captivates visitors with its intricate corridors and hidden sanctuaries.

- Ta Prohm: Famously known as the "Tomb Raider Temple," Ta Prohm is a picturesque example of the battle between nature and architecture. Towering trees and massive roots have intertwined with the temple's structure.

- Banteay Srei: This small but exquisite temple, dedicated to the god Shiva, is celebrated for its intricate red sandstone carvings, known for their intricate detail and intricate patterns.

- Preah Khan: This vast and largely unrestored temple offers a sense of adventure and exploration as visitors can wander through its corridors and courtyards.

- Banteay Samré: Known for its intricate bas-reliefs, this temple is a gem that often sees fewer visitors, making it a peaceful place to explore.

The Enigmatic Legacy:

The temples of Angkor represent not only a testament to the remarkable architectural and artistic achievements of the Khmer Empire but also serve as a symbolic representation of Cambodia itself. These temples have endured centuries, witnessing the rise and fall of empires, yet they remain a testament to the enduring spirit of the Khmer people.

Visiting Angkor Wat and the Angkor Temples is a journey through time, culture, and spirituality. It's an opportunity to immerse oneself in the mysteries of a bygone era and appreciate the beauty and significance of these architectural masterpieces that continue to captivate and inspire visitors from around the world.

Other Temple Complexes

Beyond the iconic Angkor Wat and the temples within the Angkor complex, Cambodia is home to several other temple complexes that offer unique and enchanting experiences. These lesser-known sites provide a glimpse into the country's rich history, culture, and architectural diversity. Let's explore some of these hidden gems:

Anteay Chhmar:

- Located in the northwest of Cambodia, Banteay Chhmar is a vast temple complex that remains relatively undiscovered by tourists. It's known for its stunning bas-reliefs, intricate carvings, and striking architecture. The temple features a massive face-tower similar to those found in Bayon temple, adding to its mystique.

Koh Ker:

- Nestled deep in the jungles of northern Cambodia, Koh Ker was once the capital of the Khmer Empire. The temple complex is a remote and archaeological treasure, with several towering prasats (temple towers) that provide breathtaking panoramic views when climbed.

Preah Vihear Temple:

- Perched atop the Dangrek Mountains near the Thai-Cambodian border, Preah Vihear is a spectacular temple that offers not only historical significance but also incredible vistas. The temple is famous for its dramatic cliff-side location and intricate stone carvings.

Phnom Kulen:

- This mountain range north of Angkor is a sacred site for Cambodians, known for its waterfalls, riverbed carvings, and the massive reclining Buddha statue. It's a place of pilgrimage and natural beauty, offering a serene escape from the hustle and bustle of the city.

Phnom Banan:

- Located near Battambang, Phnom Banan is a small temple complex perched on a hill, offering lovely views of the surrounding countryside. The temple's architecture is reminiscent of Angkor Wat, making it an intriguing historical site to explore.

Wat Ek Phnom:

- This temple, situated near the town of Battambang, is known for its elegant carvings and serene atmosphere. It's less crowded than the temples in Siem Reap, making it an ideal destination for those seeking a peaceful and contemplative experience.

Sambor Prei Kuk:

- Sambor Prei Kuk, also known as Isanapura, is a pre-Angkorian temple complex and a UNESCO World Heritage site. It's famed for its elegant and well-preserved structures, displaying unique brickwork and carvings.

Prasat Phnom Rung:

- This temple complex is located in northeast Cambodia and resembles the style of Angkor Wat, with beautiful lintels, sculptures, and panoramic views. It's one of the best-preserved Khmer temples outside of Cambodia.

Cambodia's Natural Beauty

Coastal Getaways

Cambodia's coastline, often overlooked in favor of its famous temples, is a hidden gem waiting to be discovered. The country's coastal getaways offer pristine beaches, charming fishing villages, and a relaxed atmosphere that contrasts with the hustle and bustle of the city. Here's an in-depth look at some of the best coastal destinations in Cambodia:

Sihanoukville:

- Once a sleepy fishing village, Sihanoukville has evolved into Cambodia's premier coastal destination. The city boasts several beautiful beaches, with Serendipity Beach and Otres Beach being popular choices. Visitors can enjoy water sports, beachside relaxation, and vibrant nightlife.

- Sihanoukville is also the gateway to nearby islands, such as Koh Rong and Koh Rong Samloem. These islands offer stunning beaches, clear waters, and a more relaxed atmosphere, perfect for those seeking a true island escape.

Kep:

- Kep, a tranquil seaside town known for its delicious seafood, is a hidden coastal gem. Visitors can explore Kep National Park, where hiking trails lead to panoramic views. The town's crumbling French colonial villas lend it a nostalgic charm.

- Don't miss the Kep Crab Market, where you can savor fresh crab dishes prepared by local vendors. Kep's blend of nature, history, and gastronomy creates a unique coastal experience.

Kampot:

- Located upstream from Kep, Kampot is another riverside town with a relaxed vibe. It's famous for its pepper plantations, which produce some of the world's finest pepper. Visitors can tour these plantations and sample the products.

- The town's picturesque riverside setting, lined with charming cafes and guesthouses, is ideal for unwinding. Bokor Mountain, with its eerie abandoned French hill station, offers an exciting day trip.

Koh Kong:

- For those seeking a more rugged and off-the-beaten-path coastal experience, Koh Kong is a prime choice. It's an emerging eco-tourism destination that showcases Cambodia's lush mangroves, waterfalls, and untamed wilderness.

- The town is a gateway to the Cardamom Mountains, one of Southeast Asia's last wilderness frontiers. Visitors can engage in jungle treks, wildlife spotting, and boat trips to explore the region's natural beauty.

Ream National Park:

- Ream National Park, situated near Sihanoukville, is a pristine coastal sanctuary rich in biodiversity. It offers a fantastic opportunity for eco-tourism, including bird watching, jungle trekking, and boat tours through mangrove forests.

- The park's sandy beaches, such as Otres Beach 2, provide a quieter alternative to Sihanoukville's busier stretches.

Tropical Rainforests and Wildlife

Cambodia's natural landscapes are rich and diverse, featuring lush tropical rainforests teeming with an incredible array of wildlife. While the country is renowned for its historic sites, its natural wonders are equally captivating. Here's an exploration of Cambodia's tropical rainforests and the remarkable wildlife that calls these ecosystems home:

1. Biodiversity Hotspot:

Cambodia's rainforests are part of the Indo-Burma biodiversity hotspot, an area known for its exceptional species diversity and endemism. The country's dense jungles and ecosystems are vital for numerous species of plants and animals.

2. Cardamom Mountains:

The Cardamom Mountains, in southwestern Cambodia, are one of the last remaining wilderness areas in Southeast Asia. These rugged, forested peaks are home to an impressive variety of wildlife, including elephants, tigers, leopards, and countless bird species.

3. Virachey National Park:

Located in northeastern Cambodia, Virachey National Park is a sprawling expanse of rainforest. It's one of Cambodia's most biodiverse areas and a critical habitat for various endangered species, such as clouded leopards, sun bears, and gibbons.

4. Diverse Flora:

Cambodia's rainforests are incredibly rich in plant species. You'll find towering hardwood trees, countless orchid species, and exotic medicinal plants that have been traditionally used by local communities.

5. Unique Primates:
Cambodia is home to various primate species, including the endangered pileated gibbon and the rare and tiny pygmy loris. These primates play a vital role in forest ecosystems and are essential for seed dispersal.

6. Conservation Efforts:
Conservation organizations, along with the Cambodian government, have been working diligently to protect these

invaluable ecosystems and the wildlife they harbor. Initiatives like the Cambodia Tiger Action Plan aim to save the critically endangered Indochinese tiger.

7. Threats to Rainforests:

Despite conservation efforts, Cambodia's rainforests are under threat from activities such as illegal logging, land conversion, and infrastructure development. These issues put immense pressure on the delicate balance of ecosystems.

8. Ecotourism Opportunities:

Ecotourism is on the rise in Cambodia, providing travelers with the chance to explore rainforests while contributing to conservation efforts. Visitors can engage in guided treks, birdwatching, and wildlife spotting tours, allowing them to witness Cambodia's natural beauty up close.

9. Sustainable Practices:

Some eco-lodges and tour operators in Cambodia are adopting sustainable and responsible practices, ensuring that tourism benefits local communities and supports conservation efforts.

10. Unique Wildlife Encounters:

Travelers to Cambodia's rainforests can encounter a remarkable array of wildlife, from the elusive Asian elephant to the vibrant plumage of various bird species, including hornbills and pittas.

Mekong River Explorations

Mekong River Explorations in Cambodia: A Journey of Natural and Cultural Wonders

The Mekong River, one of the world's great waterways, winds its way through six countries in Southeast Asia, including Cambodia. Exploring the Mekong River in Cambodia offers a unique opportunity to discover the country's natural beauty, traditional culture, and the timeless rhythm of river life. Here's an in-depth look at Mekong River explorations in Cambodia:

1. The Mighty Mekong:

The Mekong River is one of the longest rivers in Asia, flowing over 4,300 kilometers through China, Myanmar, Laos, Thailand, Cambodia, and Vietnam. In Cambodia, it plays a vital role in the country's culture, economy, and daily life.

2. Siem Reap - Gateway to Angkor Wat:

The Mekong River is not only a waterway but also a source of life for the region. It flows through Siem Reap, the gateway to the renowned Angkor Wat complex. You can explore the riverbanks of Siem Reap, visit floating villages, and learn about local fishing traditions.

3. Chaktomuk, the Confluence:

In Phnom Penh, the Mekong River meets the Tonlé Sap River at the Chaktomuk confluence. The city's iconic riverfront area is a vibrant place for a leisurely stroll and to observe daily life along the riverbanks.

4. Tonlé Sap Lake:

The Tonlé Sap Lake, connected to the Mekong River, is the largest freshwater lake in Southeast Asia. Its size fluctuates dramatically with the seasons, expanding during the monsoon and contracting in the dry season. Explore floating villages, witness traditional fishing techniques, and observe the unique way of life of the people who call this lake home.

5. Birdwatching and Wildlife:

The Mekong River basin in Cambodia is a crucial habitat for various bird species, including the critically endangered giant ibis. The river's lush surroundings are a haven for birdwatching enthusiasts and wildlife lovers.

6. Ecotourism and River Cruises:

River cruises along the Mekong River offer travelers a unique perspective on

Cambodia's landscapes, cultures, and traditions. These cruises often include stops at historical and cultural sites, as well as opportunities for excursions to local villages.

7. Floating Villages:

The floating villages along the Mekong and Tonlé Sap are a unique feature of Cambodian life. Visiting these villages provides insights into how communities adapt to the ever-changing water levels of the river.

8. Fishing Traditions:

The Mekong River is central to Cambodia's fishing industry. Observing traditional fishing practices, including the use of handmade fish traps and bamboo fish baskets, offers a glimpse into the vital role of the river in Cambodian culture.

9. Waterfront Markets:

Explore the bustling riverfront markets, where locals buy and sell everything from fresh produce to handicrafts. It's an excellent place to immerse yourself in Cambodia's daily life and discover regional specialties.

10. Cultural Encounters:

Along the Mekong, you'll have opportunities to engage with local communities and experience their cultural traditions, including local cuisine, dance, and crafts.

National Parks and Reserves

Cambodia, known for its rich cultural heritage, is also home to an array of national parks and reserves that protect the country's natural wonders. These areas showcase Cambodia's breathtaking landscapes, diverse ecosystems, and unique wildlife. Here's an in-depth look at the national parks and reserves that contribute to the preservation of Cambodia's natural beauty:

1. Virachey National Park:

Located in northeastern Cambodia, Virachey National Park is one of the country's largest and most biodiverse protected areas. It covers lush rainforests, rugged mountains, and pristine rivers. The park is home to rare and endangered species like the clouded leopard, sun bear, and gibbons.

It offers challenging treks for adventurous travelers.

2. Cardamom Mountains:

The Cardamom Mountains in southwestern Cambodia represent one of the last untouched wilderness areas in Southeast Asia. This vast expanse of tropical rainforest is teeming with wildlife, including Asian elephants, tigers, leopards, and a remarkable range of bird species. Conservation efforts are crucial in preserving this valuable ecosystem.

3. Ream National Park:

Located near Sihanoukville, Ream National Park is a coastal haven that encompasses both marine and terrestrial environments. Visitors can explore mangrove forests, diverse bird habitats, and sandy beaches. The park is a significant nesting site for various bird species, such as the endangered Milky Stork.

4. Bokor National Park:

Perched atop the Bokor Mountain near Kampot, this park offers a unique blend of natural beauty and historical intrigue. The park is home to lush forests, scenic viewpoints, and an eerie, abandoned French colonial hill station that adds a fascinating layer to the park's charm.

5. Preah Monivong Bokor National Park:

This park, located near Kampot, covers 1,500 square kilometers of varied landscapes. It is known for its unique limestone formations and the critically endangered Sunda Pangolin. The park offers opportunities for trekking, birdwatching, and wildlife spotting.

6. Kirirom National Park:

Kirirom, located in the Elephant Mountains of southwest Cambodia, is a highland sanctuary with pine forests, waterfalls, and serene lakes. Visitors can explore hiking trails, go horseback riding, and camp amidst the cool mountain air.

7. Botum Sakor National Park:

This coastal park in southwestern Cambodia comprises pristine rainforests, mangroves, and estuaries. It is a critical habitat for several endangered species, including the Asian elephant and the pileated gibbon. The park's diverse ecosystems make it a haven for wildlife enthusiasts.

8. Peam Krasaop Wildlife Sanctuary:

Situated along the southwestern coast, this sanctuary protects critical mangrove habitats and is a vital breeding ground for various fish species and bird colonies, including the globally endangered Sarus Crane.

9. Wildlife Sanctuaries:

Cambodia also has several wildlife sanctuaries, such as Phnom Prich Wildlife Sanctuary and Kulen Promtep Wildlife Sanctuary, which are essential for the conservation of endangered species and biodiversity.

10. Conservation Initiatives:

Conservation organizations, government agencies, and local communities work together to protect these natural areas. Efforts include anti-poaching measures, habitat restoration, and wildlife research.

Cambodian Culture and Traditions

Traditional Arts and Dance

Cambodia's traditional arts and dance are a testament to the country's rich cultural heritage and deep-rooted traditions. These artistic expressions, with their intricate movements, vibrant costumes, and historical significance, play a crucial role in preserving and showcasing the beauty of Cambodian culture. Here's an in-depth exploration of traditional arts and dance in Cambodia:

1. A Glimpse into the Past:
Cambodia's traditional arts and dance have a history dating back centuries. They are closely intertwined with the country's spiritual, social, and historical narratives. These artistic forms provide a window into

Cambodia's storied past, offering insights into the Khmer Empire and the influence of Hinduism and Buddhism on the culture.

2. Khmer Classical Dance:

Khmer classical dance, also known as Apsara dance, is one of Cambodia's most famous art forms. It is characterized by intricate hand gestures, graceful movements, and vibrant costumes. Apsara dancers, traditionally female, often perform stories from Hindu epics like the Ramayana and the Mahabharata.

3. Robam Preah Reach Trop:

Robam Preah Reach Trop, or the Royal Ballet of Cambodia, is a dance form that has been preserved for centuries within the royal court. This dance form involves highly trained dancers who perform elaborate and symbolic routines that reflect Cambodia's spiritual and historical narratives.

4. Shadow Puppetry (Sbaek Thom):
Cambodian shadow puppetry is an ancient art that uses leather puppets to cast shadows on a screen. Traditional stories and fables are portrayed through intricate puppet movements. Shadow puppetry often serves as a

medium for imparting moral lessons and cultural tales.

5. Traditional Music (Pinpeat and Mahori):

Accompanying traditional dance, Pinpeat and Mahori ensembles provide live music with traditional instruments such as the xylophone, drums, and string instruments. The music adds depth and emotion to the dance performances.

6. Folk Dance and Music:

Cambodia's rich cultural diversity is reflected in its many folk dances and musical traditions. These are often linked to local festivals, weddings, and communal celebrations. Folk dances, like Robam Choun Por, often involve dynamic and lively movements.

7. Preservation and Revival:
Cambodia's traditional arts and dance faced significant challenges during the Khmer Rouge regime, which sought to erase cultural expressions. However, since then, there have been concerted efforts to revive and preserve these traditions. Organizations and schools now work to teach and pass on these cultural treasures to new generations.

8. The Living Arts:

Phare, the Cambodian Circus, is an excellent example of a contemporary arts initiative that merges traditional and modern forms of expression. The circus showcases the talent of Cambodian youth while promoting cultural awareness.

9. UNESCO Recognition:

Cambodia's traditional arts and dance, particularly Apsara dance, were recognized by UNESCO as an Intangible Cultural Heritage of Humanity, highlighting their global significance.

10. Cultural Identity:

Traditional arts and dance are an integral part of Cambodian identity, reflecting the resilience, creativity, and spirituality of the Khmer people. They provide a cultural anchor in a rapidly changing world.

Exploring Cambodia's traditional arts and dance is an enchanting journey that immerses visitors in the heart and soul of the country. These art forms are not only a source of pride but also a means of passing down cultural values, stories, and aesthetics to future generations. Cambodia's vibrant expressions of art and dance continue to captivate and inspire, ensuring that the country's rich cultural legacy endures for years to come.

Festivals and Events

Cambodians, like most people, appreciate any excuse to throw a party, and they know how to do it in style. It's amazing to visit the country during festivals like the Water Festival and Khmer New Year and join the people in dancing, drinking, singing, and praying. Cambodian holidays are an excellent opportunity to unwind and appreciate the vivid culture of this dynamic Asian country.

Chaul Chnam Chen (Chinese New Year) and Tet (Vietnamese New Year)

Depending on the year, Chinese and Vietnamese New Year celebrations take place in late January or early February. Even though Cambodia celebrates its new year a few months later, these events remain popular. This is especially true in Phnom Penh, where Chinese entrepreneurs dominate the business scene. The bulk of businesses are closed for the duration, and there are various street celebrations.

Chaul Chnam Khmer

The biggest and most hectic event of the year, Khmer New Year, begins in the middle of April. It's a fantastic time to visit the nation and enjoy the pleasures of life, and even though April has the harshest sun, chances are the locals will enjoy dousing you with talcum powder and water on a daily basis. While many people in Phnom Penh travel to the provinces to visit family, there is plenty going on in the city, particularly at Wat Phnom and on the Royal Palace grounds, where people of all ages congregate to enjoy the festival.

Chat Preah Nengkal (Royal Ploughing Ceremony)

The Royal Ploughing Ceremony, a yearly agricultural ritual held in early May to decide how plentiful the crop will be, is one of the kingdom's most unusual days. The royal family leads the royal oxen on the lawn outside the National Museum in Phnom Penh, who auspiciously inform the assembled multitude on the outcome of their harvest. A strange but fascinating ritual!

Visakha Puja (Buddha Day)

Visakha Puja, one of Cambodia's holiest holidays, commemorates the Buddha's life from conception to enlightenment and, finally, death. The occasion is observed at temples around the country on the eighth day of the fourth moon. Witnessing the festival at Angkor Wat is especially worthwhile, as hundreds of monks form a lighted procession.

P'Chum Ben (Festival of the Dead)

A Buddhist All Souls' Day is an odd festival in which the living honour the dead. People who are deeply superstitious visit temples and contribute candles, food, flowers, and paper money. During the ritual, Buddhist devotees are expected to visit seven temples, which will be mediated by monks.

Bon Om Tuk (Water Festival)

During Water Festival, the entire country descends on the capital and other major cities for what is undoubtedly Cambodia's biggest celebration. One of the most important events of the year, Bon Om Tuk, recalls the god-king Jayavarman's heroic expulsion out of Angkor of the Cham

invaders in 1177. The cities are alive
with live music, food booths, sellers,
and a celebratory atmosphere, while
hundreds of brilliantly painted boats
compete in large river races. If you plan
to attend, it is strongly advised that you
reserve a room well in advance.

Things to Do in Cambodia

Most visitors to Cambodia visit either
the historic lanes of Phnom Penh, with
its Royal Palace and bustling nightlife,
or the temples around Siem Reap,

which is home to the world-famous Angkor Wat. However, there is much more going on in the kingdom than meets the eye.

Explore the mountains and waterfalls of the frigid northern areas of Mondulkiri and Ratanakiri. Along the way, look for the virtually extinct Irrawaddy dolphin and make plans to bathe former working elephants. Preah Vihear temple, the pinnacle of Angkorian luxury, is open for visitation again now that the military standoff with Thailand has resolved. There are numerous tour companies in all of Cambodia's major cities who can assist you with your travels and provide a detailed description of what you're seeing.

Outside of Siem Reap, temple-hopping is a great treat, whether you choose to see a handful in a single day or spend an entire week viewing them all. The region that was once the heart of the Khmer Empire is home to a number of religious complexes, including the massive Angkor Wat, the world's largest religious structure, and the long-lost jungle temples made famous by Laura Croft. Angkor Tour Guides provide a variety of different-length trips around the Angkor temples.

An eco-tour operator, Mekong Discovery Trail, provides some of the best vistas into Cambodia's northeastern heartland, where you can learn about life on the enormous river. Environmental tours provide a unique opportunity to explore true Cambodia, whether you opt to kayak through waterlogged woods, climb to abandoned temples, or get up close and personal with the nearly extinct Irrawaddy dolphin at Kratie.

Jeep trips are an excellent opportunity to get away from the city and explore the surrounding countryside. Beetlenut

Tours, based in Phnom Penh, specialising in tours to the Phnom Tamao wildlife Rescue Centre, where you may eat a Khmer lunch while viewing a variety of indigenous species such as elephants, tigers, gibbons, and sun bears.

Even if the recently built five-star hotel is changing the image of the once deserted Bokor Mountain, trekking this scary ghost town is still a fantastic experience. The Bokor Palace Hotel and Casino, the King's old residence, was once a luxury hangout for the local elite but is now a dilapidated monument with bullet holes from the Khmer

Rouge era. Sok Lim Tours organises day tours to Bokor from neighbouring Kampot.

Cambodia's bamboo train is perhaps one of Asia's most exhilarating and distinctive train journeys. This train, known as a norry in Cambodian, has a petrol engine, is totally made of bamboo and wood, and can carry up to 15 passengers. Despite the fact that the country only has one track, true trains are hard to come by and move slowly, giving you plenty of time to get to know your fellow passengers. Battambang Tour may organise these specialised tours.

Virachay National Park is one of the top trekking destinations in Cambodia, with stunning scenery. Hikes are one of the most appealing ways to visit the country's most remote locations; they range in length. The 3,325 square metre park in Ratanakiri Province is home to spectacular jungle and meandering rivers, as well as a plethora of animals such as tigers, leopards, bears, and gibbons. Trips may be organised by Yaklom Hill Londge and Terres Rouges, two local establishments.

Diving and snorkelling off the coast of Sihanoukville is a popular way to pass the time while discovering some of the magnificent corals, sponges, and marine life near the shore, including eels, stingrays, and dolphins. The best diving spots are on the islands of Koh Tas and Koh Rung Samloem, which may also be reached by overnight boat. The Dive Shop Cambodia handles equipment rentals and tour bookings.

Shopping and Leisure in Cambodia

Unlike many other Southeast Asian towns, the capital of Cambodia has only recently witnessed the emergence of retail malls; nonetheless, don't expect anything like the air-conditioned shopping complexes found back home or in Bangkok. Visit one of the many street markets instead, and allow yourself to be enchanted by the enormous selection of silks, antiques, and handicrafts available. In most markets in Southeast Asia, bartering is the norm. Never take the first price that is given, don't be overly interested in something, even if you really want it, and keep the process informal and enjoyable.

Psah Tmhey (Central Market), in the capital, is still a well-known destination for shoppers in Cambodia.

It is a remarkable example of Art Deco architecture, built by the French in the 1930s. It is one of the main tourist destinations in Phnom Penh due to the wide range of things available at reasonable prices. This brightly coloured, ostentatious dome offers everything from cheap Levis, electronic goods, and flowers to Chinese coins, swords, and handicrafts.

One thing to be wary of at Phnom Penh's markets is the abundance of low-cost brand-name apparel. Some products get lost in the cracks in an economy dominated by clothing and wind up being sold for a fraction of what you would pay at home. However, the most alluring aspect of shopping in Cambodia is its renowned silk and textiles, a large portion of which are still woven by hand and coloured naturally. This is one of the best places to shop for premium textiles because most silk fields are close to Siem Reap.

In Cambodia, sculpture is a major industry, with people continuing the highly regarded practise of their ancestors. Shops across numerous avenues sell stone sculptures of Buddhas, Jayavarman VI, and Hindu deities in a variety of sizes, quality ranges, and pricing points. Another significant aspect of Cambodian culture is woodcarving. Once more, there are several replicas of Buddhas and gods that are excellent gifts to bring home. The markets also have a lot of antiquities, but bear in mind that counterfeit goods are common in this part of the world, so always thoroughly inspect your purported deal before making a purchase.

Food and Restaurants In Cambodia

Phnom Penh has gained a strong reputation in recent years for both the quantity and quality of food offered in restaurants and for its vibrant nightlife in the heart of the BKK1 district and along the bustling riverbank. Cambodia's capital is full of mid-to high-end French restaurants, authentic pizzerias, quirky tapas bars, and an abundance of Asian restaurants, from budget-friendly Indian curry houses to luxurious Korean BBQ locations, all thanks to its Franco-colonial past. However, as of right now, neither Burger King nor the omnipresent McDonald's are mentioned. Visit the Khmer barbecue and beer gardens for a more genuine experience. A meal of spit roast beef, fried rice and a jug of the local beer, Angkor, will cost you slightly more than $5. Similar and smaller-scale cuisines are offered by other popular tourist destinations, including as Sihanoukville and Siem Reap; but, outside of these cities, you're likely to find just local options.

Bars and Pubbing in Cambodia

There are many different types of bars in Phnom Penh, Sihanoukville, and Siem Reap, though the latter is still the hub for backpackers. Depending on the establishment, there are wide variations in the operating hours. The place to be in Phnom Penh is the well-known Riverside (Sisowath Quay), especially in the early evening when many bars, even the upscale ones, provide happy hour specials. While Equinox (3A Street 278, Phnom Penh) draws music and dance enthusiasts with a wide selection of bands and salsa evenings, Cafe Metro (corner of Sisowath Quay and Street 148, Phnom Penh) is a sophisticated hangout with an extensive drink menu.

As the beach party town of Cambodia, Sihanoukville lives up to its reputation. Many bars line the town's beaches, including the colourful Aquarium (Serendipity Beach, Sihanoukville), which regularly features live blues and country acts, and the peculiar Russian-owned Airport (Victory Hill, Sihanoukville), which is a diner turned disco with reasonably priced food and drinks.

Visit Angkor What? (Pub Street, Siem Reap), the town's original pub, after a tiring day of touring temples. Here, you may share tales from your journey. Alternatively, the décor and atmosphere of Miss Wong (The Lane, Siem Reap) can whisk you back in time to 1920s Shanghai.

Dining and Cuisine in Cambodia

The city's many well-established French restaurants, including La Croisette (Sisowath Quay, Phnom Penh), one of the international diners with the longest history in the kingdom, have been joined by the burgeoning culinary scene in recent years. Rahu (Phnom Penh's Sisowath Quay) is yet another excellent Riverside location. It is a favorite of both foreigners and members of Cambodia's emerging upper class, serving delicious fusion dinners of Japanese and Khmer cuisine. Dolce Italia, a recent addition to Phnom Penh's culinary scene, is located on Sothearos Boulevard and serves classic Italian pizzas made by the restaurant's Sicilian chef.

Although Siem Reap and Sihanoukville don't have as good of food as Phnom Penh, they do have a few really good restaurants. Delicious meals can be found at the majestic FCC Angkor (River Road, Siem Reap), which is housed in a grand colonial building. Sugar Palm (Taphul Street, Siem Reap) is well-known for its trademark dish, char kroeng, a lemongrass curry, and exquisite atmosphere.

Sihanoukville has a lot of cheap restaurants, but it also has some really good ones. For example, New Sea View Villa (Serendipity Street, Sihanoukville) offers excellent French food, and Happa (Serendipity Road, Sihanoukville) is a teppanyaki joint that serves Japanese favorites along with tempura and sashimi.

Getting Around Cambodia

Transportation Options

There are a number of ways to travel to Cambodia, including by plane, bus, train, and car.

By plane

The most convenient way to travel to Cambodia is by plane. The country has three international airports: Phnom Penh International Airport (PNH), Siem Reap International Airport (REP), and Sihanoukville International Airport

(KOS). There are a number of international airlines that offer direct flights to Cambodia, including Qatar Airways, Emirates, Singapore Airlines, and Thai Airways.

By bus

There are a number of bus companies that offer bus services to Cambodia from neighboring countries such as Thailand, Vietnam, and Laos. The journey time will vary depending on your departure point, but it can take up to 24 hours to travel to Cambodia by bus.

By train

There is a train service that operates between Phnom Penh and Bangkok, Thailand. The train journey takes around 15 hours.

By car

It is possible to drive to Cambodia from neighboring countries such as Thailand and Vietnam. However, it is important to note that the roads in Cambodia can be in poor condition, and traffic can be heavy. It is also important to have a valid driver's license and insurance.

Airports In Cambodia

Phnom Penh International Airport

The airport in Phnom Penh serves as both the principal entry point into the country and the busiest airport in Cambodia, with over 1.5 million passengers traveling through it each year. Domestic Cambodia Angkor Air flights to Siem Reap are available, as are regional flights to Ho Chi Minh City (Saigon) and multiple connections to significant regional destinations. Other notable airlines that use this airport include AirAsia, Vietnam Airlines,

Bangkok Air, and Air France. Bangkok, Seoul, Shanghai, Beijing, Singapore, and Kuala Lumpur are all key transportation hubs in the region.

There are several internationally recognised eateries at the airport, such as Dairy Queen and The Pizza Company, but there are also several duty-free shops, such as EZI Wear and Travel, Ambre Boutique, and Dufry Cambodia. There are always cabs and tuk-tuks waiting outside the airport to take you to the city core, which is about a 30-minute drive away.

Siem Reap International Airport

The Siem Reap airport, which serves as the gateway to Angkor Wat and the other temples, averages 1.5 million passengers per year. Cambodia Angkor Air operates domestic flights from the airports of Phnom Penh and Sihanoukville. A variety of regional airlines, including AirAsia, SilkAir, and Vietnam Air, fly to and from Phnom Penh International Airport in Siem Reap. However, no direct flights from Europe are accepted.

The airport has only a café, a Dairy Queen, and a duty-free shop owned by the neighbouring corporation Attwood. The six-kilometer drive from the airport to Siem Reap is not covered by specialised ground transportation, but you can easily catch a taxi or tuk-tuk to get into the city.

Sihanoukville International Airport

The third airport in Cambodia, also known as Preah Sihanouk Airport and Kang Keng Airport, is located 11 miles (18 kilometers) east of town. Despite being built with Soviet assistance in the

1960s, the airport was virtually abandoned during and after the American Civil War. It reopened in December 2011 and is now operated by Cambodia Angkor Air, which operates a triweekly service from Sihanoukville. Tuk-tuks, traditional taxis, and motorbike taxis run between the beach town and the airport.

Navigating Cambodia

Cambodia Taxis and Car Rental

Metered taxis are still extremely rare on the roadways, even though hailing one in Phnom Penh and other big cities is getting more and more convenient. Accommodations can book a cab or a private car for the day, though there aren't many firms that operate, so you won't be able to flag one down on the street. A shared cab or minibus can be used for long-distance transportation. While Siem Reap Taxi Service (+855-979-330-300) is located in and around Siem Reap, Car Rental Co, Ltd (+855-23-880-001) is located in Phnom Penh.

Cambodia, Moto Taxis and Tuk-Tuks

Whether riding on the back of a motorcycle (known locally as a moto, moto taxi or motodop) or in a tuk-tuk, a small motorcycle with an attached carriage, is the most popular and fun method to go around towns and cities in Cambodia. While they blend in with the crowd when riding a motorbike, moto drivers are always present and will take every opportunity to draw attention to themselves. You will pay a little bit extra for a tuk-tuk, particularly if there are several of you. Setting a price is usually a good idea before you leave.

Cambodia buses and trains

Although there are now no passenger trains in operation in Cambodia, the country's rail network connecting it to China and Singapore is scheduled for repair at some point. Conversely, buses are a well-liked means of transit between cities. Private operators run buses to and from important domestic and regional destinations, even though there are no municipal bus networks inside the cities. The buses range in quality, however they are typically extremely reasonably priced. It's usually only a few bucks that separate a pleasant eight-hour journey from a miserable one, so it's always worthwhile to choose for the most comfortable option. Both Phnom Penh Sorya Transport Co, Ltd (+855-23-240-359) and GST Express Bus (+855-12-895-550) provide a decent service and operate on a range of domestic routes.

Cambodia boats

Because of significant road improvements in recent years, boats—which were formerly necessary for travelling around Cambodia—are being utilised less frequently. On the other hand, one of the most picturesque ways to see the kingdom is still taking a leisurely ride down the vast Mekong. One of the most well-liked boat tours for visitors is the six-hour trip from Phnom Penh to Siem Reap, which VietVision Travel (+855-12-498-599) offers daily throughout the dry season (October to April).

Practical Travel Tips

If you are entering Cambodia via air and require a visa, make sure to fill out all the required documentation before arrival, as the visa desk can become rather hectic and disorganized

- When traveling in a tuk-tuk or moto taxi, it is always a good idea to carry a map, as drivers usually have limited English and tend to nod eagerly regardless of whether they know your destination or not

- When traveling in the provinces, or around temples, make sure to stick to the designated paths, as many areas in rural Cambodia are still littered with land mines
- It's always useful to rent a helmet if you plan to travel via moto taxis

Contact Numbers

Police: 117 Emergency: 117 (police), 118 (fire), 119 (ambulance) Royal Rattanat Hospital: +855-23-986-992 US Embassy: +855-23-427-124 UK

Embassy: +855-23-427-124 Australian
Embassy: +855-23-213-470 Car Rental
Co, Ltd: +855-23-880-001

Meeting the Locals

Interacting with Cambodians

When you visit Cambodia, you'll quickly discover that the warmth and friendliness of the Cambodian people are among the country's most treasured assets. Interacting with Cambodians is an opportunity to engage with a vibrant culture, learn about the country's history, and form meaningful connections. Here are some tips on how to navigate social interactions in the Kingdom of Wonder:

1. Greetings:

-Greetings are important: Cambodians value respectful and polite greetings. A simple "sua s'dei" (hello) or "chum reap sua" (good morning) can go a long way in opening doors to friendly interactions.

-Use the traditional greeting: When meeting someone for the first time or in a formal setting, it's customary to place your hands together in a prayer-like gesture and bow slightly while saying "chum reap sua."

2. Be Respectful:

- Show respect to elders: In Cambodian culture, respect for elders is paramount. When addressing someone older than you, use polite honorifics like "bong" for an older brother or sister, "lok ta" for an older man, and "lok yeay" for an older woman.

3. Smile and Be Friendly:

-The "Land of Smiles": Cambodia is often referred to as the "Land of Smiles," and its people are known for their warmth. A friendly demeanor, including a smile and open body language, is an excellent way to engage with locals.

4. Learn Some Khmer Phrases:

- Learn a few basic Khmer phrases: While English is spoken in urban areas, making an effort to speak a few Khmer words and phrases can greatly enhance your interactions and show respect for the local culture.

5. Show Interest in Cambodian Culture:

-Ask questions: Cambodians are proud of their culture, so asking questions about traditions, festivals, and customs can lead to interesting conversations. Cambodians are often delighted to share their heritage.

6. Be Mindful of Cultural Sensitivities:

- Religious sites: When visiting temples or religious sites, dress modestly, remove your shoes before entering, and be mindful of quiet and respectful behavior.

- Head and feet: In Cambodian culture, the head is considered the most sacred part of the body, while the feet are the least. Avoid touching someone's head and never point your feet at people or religious objects.

7. Engage in Local Activities:

- Participate in local customs: Joining in local customs, such as offering alms to monks in the morning or celebrating local festivals, can be a memorable way to connect with Cambodians.

8. Be Generous with Compliments:

-Compliment their country: Cambodians take pride in their homeland. Compliments about the beauty of Cambodia, its history, or its culture are often well-received.

9. Accept Invitations:

-Hospitality: Cambodians are known for their hospitality and may invite you to their homes. Accepting such invitations is a way to immerse yourself in local life and build lasting friendships.

10. Be Patient:

-Time: Cambodians have a more relaxed sense of time, so it's important to be patient in your interactions. Delays and waiting are common, but it's all part of the cultural experience.

Homestays and Local Experiences

When visiting Cambodia, choosing homestays and seeking out local experiences offers a unique opportunity to immerse yourself in the authentic culture of this enchanting country. These experiences provide a glimpse into the daily lives, traditions, and hospitality of the Khmer people, fostering a deep connection with the local way of life. Here's a closer look at homestays and local experiences in Cambodia:

1. Authentic Cultural Immersion:

- Homestays provide a genuine cultural exchange, allowing you to live and share experiences with Cambodian families. This immersion offers insights into the traditions, values, and customs that shape Khmer society.

2. Warm Cambodian Hospitality:

- Cambodians are known for their warmth and friendliness. Staying with a local family provides first hand experience of their hospitality. You'll be welcomed with open arms and treated as an honored guest.

3. Home-Cooked Khmer Cuisine:

- One of the highlights of a homestay is savoring homemade Khmer dishes. You can join in the preparation or simply relish the flavors of traditional Cambodian meals. It's a chance to taste authentic dishes that may not be readily available in restaurants.

4. Sharing Stories and Traditions:

- Homestay hosts often enjoy sharing stories about their family, customs, and the local community. This can lead to rich cultural exchanges and deepen your understanding of Cambodia.

5. Rural and Urban Experiences:

- Cambodia offers a range of homestay options, from rural villages to urban areas. Whether you want to experience the simple life of a countryside village or the vibrancy of city living, there's a homestay experience to suit your preferences.

6. Unique Activities:

- Homestays often include opportunities for participating in daily activities, such as farming, fishing, or crafting. You can join locals in their routines, gaining a newfound appreciation for their way of life.

7. Community Involvement:

- By staying in a homestay, you contribute to the economic well-being of the local community. The income generated through homestays often supports education, infrastructure, and other community development projects.

8. Responsible Tourism:

- Homestays are an example of responsible tourism, allowing travelers to engage with local culture in a respectful and sustainable way. The income generated directly benefits the host families and their communities.

9. Local Guides:

- In many cases, you'll have local guides or hosts who can show you around the area and introduce you to nearby attractions, such as temples, markets, or natural wonders.

10. Memorable Connections:

- The relationships formed during homestays can be some of the most cherished memories of your trip. These connections often lead to a deeper appreciation of Cambodia's rich cultural tapestry.

Understanding Khmer Hospitality

Cambodia, often referred to as the "Land of Smiles," is a country renowned not only for its stunning landscapes and rich history but also for the genuine warmth and hospitality of its people. Khmer hospitality is deeply ingrained in the culture, and understanding it is key to experiencing the true essence of Cambodia. Here's an in-depth look at Khmer hospitality and the values that underpin it:

1. Open Arms and Warm Smiles:
- Khmer hospitality is characterized by open arms and warm, welcoming smiles. Cambodians have a genuine and heartfelt desire to make visitors feel comfortable and appreciated.

2. Generosity and Sharing:

- Cambodians are known for their generosity, and it's common for them to go out of their way to offer food, drink, or assistance to guests. Sharing is a fundamental aspect of Khmer hospitality, whether it's a meal, a drink, or simply a kind gesture.

3. Family-Centered:

- Family is the cornerstone of Khmer society, and hospitality often revolves around the family unit. Guests are treated like family members, and their well-being is of paramount importance.

4. Politeness and Respect:

- Politeness and respect are integral to Khmer culture. Greetings, such as the "sompiah" (a slight bow and hands together), show respect for others. When interacting with Cambodians, using polite language and showing respect for local customs is appreciated.

5. Offering Assistance:

- Cambodians are always ready to offer assistance or guidance to visitors. If you need directions, help with language, or information about local customs, don't hesitate to ask.

6. Humility and Humbleness:

- Cambodians often exhibit a sense of humility and humbleness. They don't boast about their own achievements but instead focus on making others feel valued and appreciated.

7. Gift Giving:

- Gift giving is a common practice in Khmer hospitality. When visiting someone's home, it's customary to bring a small gift, such as fruit or sweets, as a token of appreciation.

8. Sharing Food:

- Khmer culture revolves around food, and sharing meals is a significant aspect of hospitality. Whether in a restaurant or a local home, Cambodians often encourage guests to partake in communal dining, further strengthening connections.

9. Respect for Elders:

- Respecting elders is a deeply ingrained cultural value. When interacting with older Cambodians, showing deference and reverence is greatly appreciated.

10. Flexibility and Adaptability:

- Cambodians are known for their flexibility and adaptability. They value a laid-back approach to life, and they often take things as they come, making it easier for visitors to immerse themselves in the local culture.

Language Tips and Common Phrases

When traveling in Cambodia, knowing some basic Khmer language tips and common phrases can greatly enhance your experience by allowing you to connect with locals and show respect for their culture. While many Cambodians in urban areas may speak some English, making an effort to speak their language can go a long way. Here are some language tips and common phrases to help you communicate effectively:

1. Greetings:
- Hello - សួស្តី (soo-s'day / chum reap sua)
- Good morning - រាជរដ្ឋប្រចាំថ្ងៃ (reach-rhat-bra-chahm-thngai)
- Good afternoon-រាជរដ្ឋព្យាយាម (reach-rhat-bra-chahm-p'yeh-s a-yam)

- Good evening - រាជរដ្ឋបុត្រយូ
  (reach-rhat-bra-chahm-buttroo)
- Good night - រាជរដ្ឋនាវាំ
  (reach-rhat-bra-chahm-naa-vaa
  m)
- How are you? - អ្នកសុខសប្បាយរ៉ូ?
  (nay sok sa-bay-rok?)
- I'm fine, thank you -
  អីអ្នកអាចស្កករ
  (okun-haa-yeay-sok-sa-bay?)

2. Basic Phrases:

- Yes - បាទ (baat)
- No - ទេ (tey)
- Please - សូម (s'maw)
- Thank you - អរគុណ (aw-koon)

- Excuse   me   –   សូមសុំរ៍
(s'maw-som-riep)
- I'm sorry - សុំរ៍ (som-riep)

3. Numbers:

- 1 - មួយ (mu-uy)
- 2 - ពីរ (pii)
- 3 - បី (bei)
- 4 - ឃូ (boo)
- 5 - ប្រាំ (prah)
- 10- ដប់ (dap)
- 20 - ម្ភៃ (mu-vay)
- 100 - រយ (roy)

4. Directions:

- Where is...? - ...នៅណា? (...naw-naa?)

- Left - ឆ្វេ (chhang)
- Right - ស្ដាំ (s'dei)
- Straight ahead - តែលើខត (tae-lee keet)

5. Food and Dining:
- Menu - ម៉ឺនុ (mey-noo)
- Water - ទឹក (tuk)
- Rice- បាយ (baay)
- Delicious - ល្អ (l'bei)
- Bill, please - លុះជ្រ (lok-groh)

6. Shopping:
- How much is this? - ប្រមាយបេតុប្យេរ (bra-maay bate-bi)

Conclusion

In the closing pages of this Cambodia Travel Guide, we find ourselves at the end of an exhilarating adventure, yet also standing on the precipice of new beginnings. The journey through the heart of this captivating nation has been a revelation, unveiling a tapestry of culture, history, and natural beauty that has left an indelible mark on our souls.

From the ancient temples of Angkor Wat, shrouded in the mists of time, to the bustling streets of Phnom Penh, each page of this guide has transported us to the heart of Cambodia's unique charm. We've explored the enchanting coastal getaways and ventured deep into the lush, untamed rainforests that shelter Cambodia's precious wildlife.

Yet, beyond the splendid landscapes and architectural marvels, this travel guide has peeled back the layers of Cambodia to reveal its cultural riches. We've witnessed the graceful movements of Apsara dancers and marveled at the captivating tales spun through shadow puppetry. We've indulged in the flavors of Khmer cuisine and relished the warmth of Cambodian hospitality. These experiences have provided us with a deeper understanding of a country where tradition meets modernity in a harmonious dance.

But Cambodia's story is not only one of enchantment and splendor; it's also a testament to resilience and rebirth. The chapters devoted to Cambodia's harrowing history, with its grim reminders of the Killing Fields and S-21 Prison, serve as stark reminders of the indomitable human spirit and the importance of preserving the memory of the past.

As our journey concludes, we realize that Cambodia is more than a destination; it's a place where history, culture, and nature converge to form an intricate mosaic. It's a land where the echoes of the past reverberate alongside the vibrant pulse of the present, reminding us that life, like Cambodia, is a tapestry woven from threads of joy and sorrow.

So, as we bid adieu to the pages of this travel guide, we stand on the threshold of a journey yet to come. Cambodia has opened its arms to us, inviting us to delve deeper into its mysteries, connect with its people, and uncover the hidden gems that lie off the beaten path. It's an invitation to embark on a transformative adventure, where the wonders of the past and the magic of the present coexist in perfect harmony.

In the end, the Cambodia Travel Guide is not just a book; it's a passport to an experience that transcends mere tourism. It's a key to unlocking the secrets of a nation where every temple, every market, and every smile carries a story waiting to be told. It's an introduction to a place where the past and the present converge, offering a profound and lasting connection that will accompany you on your journey long after you've closed the final chapter.

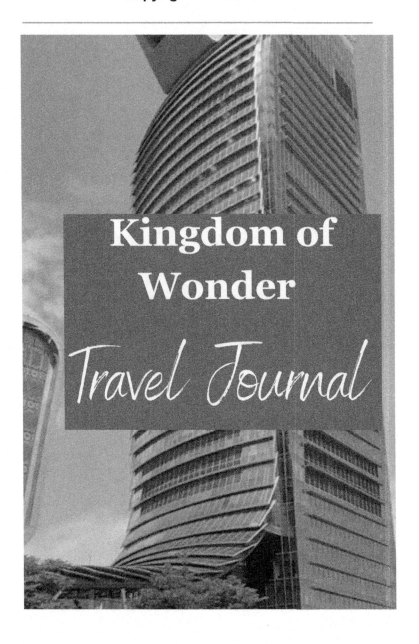

Kingdom of
Wonder

Travel Journal

Cambodia *Journal*
Travel

To do List

_____

_____

_____

_____

I'm grateful for..

_____

_____

_____

_____

_____

_____

Cambodia
Travel
Journal

To do List

_____

_____

_____

_____

I'm grateful for..

_____

_____

_____

_____

_____

Cambodia *Journal*
Travel

To do List

_____

_____

_____

_____

I'm grateful for..

_____

_____

_____

_____

_____

_____

Cambodia **Journal**
Travel

Daily Note

To do List

_____

_____

_____

_____

I'm grateful for..

_____

_____

_____

_____

_____

_____

Cambodia *Journal*
Travel

Daily Note

To do List

_____

_____

_____

_____

_____

I'm grateful for..

_____

_____

_____

_____

_____

_____

Cambodia
Travel *Journal*

To do List

I'm grateful for..

Cambodia Travel *Journal*

Daily Note

To do List

I'm grateful for..

Cambodia **Journal**
Travel

To do List

_____

_____

_____

_____

I'm grateful for..

_____

_____

_____

_____

_____

_____

Cambodia *Journal*
Travel

To do List

_____

_____

_____

_____

I'm grateful for..

_____

_____

_____

_____

_____

With love

From Meredith

Printed in Great Britain
by Amazon

36635859R00126